MW01041530

SCIENCE FOR KIDS

Dinosaurs

God's Mysterious Creatures

SCIENCE FOR KIDS

Dinosaurs

God's Mysterious Creatures

Illustrated by Susan Windsor

INSTITUTE FOR CREATION RESEARCH

Dallas, Texas
ICR.org

SCIENCE FOR KIDS

Dinosaurs
God's Mysterious Creatures

First printing: May 2017

Copyright © 2017 by the Institute for Creation Research. All rights reserved. No portion of this book may be used in any form without written permission of the publisher, with the exception of brief excerpts in articles and reviews. For more information, write to Institute for Creation Research, P. O. Box 59029, Dallas, TX 75229.

All Scripture quotations are from the New King James Version.

ISBN: 978-1-935587-93-4
Library of Congress Catalog Number: 2017937075

Please visit our website for other books and resources: ICR.org

Printed in the United States of America.

Table of Contents

Dinosaurs at Creation

Have you heard the tale of how it all began? And when I say "all," I mean ALL. Everything that ever existed. Everything we can see—like water, clouds, and our two big toes. And everything we can't see—like the air we breathe, the earth's core, and our beating hearts. The Bible tells how it all began. How God created everything in the sky and on the earth, visible and invisible, in only six days. Wow! That's less than one week!

On Day 6, He created all the land animals—that includes dinosaurs! He also created the first people: Adam and Eve. And the Bible's timeline shows this creation week happened only thousands of years ago.

Day 1: Light

Day 2: Waters

Day 3: Dry Land

Day 4: Sun, Moon, Stars

Day 5: Sea Animals and Birds

Day 6: Land Animals and Humans

Dinos and the Fall

All of God's creation was perfect. Animals and people lived in harmony, the world overflowed with beauty, and no one died. There were no funerals, hospitals, weapons, or cages because no one needed them. But all of that changed when Adam and Eve stopped trusting the God who made them. Eve ate fruit from a tree in their garden that God told them not to eat. And Adam took a bite, too.

We call this "the Fall" of humans.

From that moment, sin entered the world and ruined every part of it. Animals fought over food and ate each other. People stopped being friends with God, their Creator. And everyone faced a big, bad, mean enemy: death.

We still see all of these sad things today. And they play a big part in the dinosaur story.

But don't worry! God has a special plan to make the world right again and to get rid of death forever. We'll talk more about His great plan later in this book.

First, let's talk about what those fascinating dinos really were.

What Is a Dinosaur?

Dinos capture our imaginations. We love to see them in movies, books, and museums. But what makes a dinosaur…well…a dinosaur?

People must have been finding dino fossils for centuries. But it wasn't until 200 years ago that they recognized dinosaurs as a new kind of animal. In the 1800s, Sir Richard Owen came up with the word Dinosauria, which means "terribly great lizard."

Dinosaurs were unique land reptiles that walked upright. God designed them in many shapes and sizes, and they walked the earth more recently than you might think.

Scientists first thought dinos crawled on their bellies like lizards. Eventually, they realized these beasts were built differently. They had a hip structure that made their legs go straight down. Their tails stuck out in the air. And they were way bigger than the lizards you see in your backyard!

All dinos fit into one of five different categories. The name of each group is a pretty big word, so let's keep it simple with an easy way to remember them:

- Sharp-Tooth Dinos (Theropoda)
- Long-Neck Dinos (Sauropodomorpha)
- Duck-Bill Dinos (Ornithopoda)
- Helmet Dinos (Marginocephalia)
- Armor Dinos (Thyreophora)

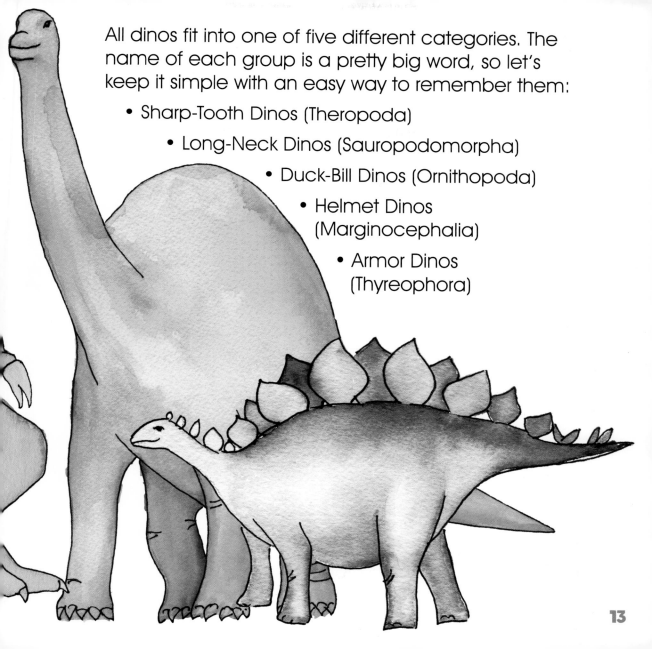

What Isn't a Dinosaur?

Many huge, extinct reptiles are mistaken for dinosaurs, but they're not really dinos at all.

The 50-foot-long plesiosaur resembles a sea monster, and the ichthyosaur had about 150 sharp teeth. But don't fall for their tricks! They're not dinosaurs—they're both marine reptiles.

Every continent, including Antarctica, has mosasaur fossils. A 50-foot mosasaur could probably eat a person in one bite. Was he a dinosaur? Nope, he's a gigantic ocean-dwelling reptile, too. Dino fact: No known dinosaurs had flippers, and it's not likely that any lived in the ocean.

And what about those high-flying pterosaurs? They were

ichthyosaur

Dimetrodon

flying reptiles with wingspans of more than 20 feet. Dino fact: No known dinosaurs had wings.

pterodactyl

We see the 10-foot *Dimetrodon* in dinosaur books and movies all the time. But he wasn't a dinosaur, either! The snaggletooth *Dimetrodon* was a reptile with legs that sprawled out from his body, but dinosaur legs extended straight down.

All of these cool creatures have some features in common with dinosaurs, and they lived on the earth at the same time. But God designed these reptiles with their own special traits that set them apart from dinosaurs.

plesiosaur

mosasaur

Plants and Animals Existed with Dinos

Have you ever heard a teacher or scientist talk about the theory of evolution? If you believe the Bible, you may wonder how evolution could be true.

Evolution says every creature formed from an original creature through small changes over millions of years. That means fish gradually turned into reptiles and then dinosaurs, which eventually turned into birds. On it went until apes turned into people. This story disagrees with the Bible's history that says God created everything in six days according to their basic kinds. That means dinos have always been dinos!

Evolutionists believe dinosaurs evolved before many other animals and plants. But many of today's creatures, like birds, reptiles, and insects, are found as fossils in the same rock layers as dinos or are even buried together with dinos.

If God created animals and plants together during the creation week, then dinosaur fossils could have mixed with many other kinds of creatures, shrubs, flowers, and trees—and that's just what we find!

Two Dino Stories

Remember what happened in the very beginning? God created dinosaurs and people on the same day only thousands of years ago. Both walked the earth at the very same time—though probably not in the same places.

But scientists who don't believe the Bible tell a different story. They say dinos lived and died millions of years before the first people ever existed.

Which dino tale tells the truth?

If dinosaurs died before the first man, Adam, sinned, then death would not be God's punishment for man's sin as the Bible says.

But we can trust the Bible because God inspired it, and He knows everything!

He tells us how the world began and where we all came from. He was there from the start! He knows how it happened and when. And as you'll see in this book, many scientific discoveries agree with what the Bible says.

Without God's Word to tell us where dinosaurs, people, and everything else came from, scientists can only make guesses based on their limited information.

Dino Dinner

When God created dinosaurs, He made them vegetarians. All were part of Team Veggie. None were Meat Lovers—not even one!

How do we know that? Well, in Genesis 1:30, God said, "To every beast of the earth, to every bird of the air, and to everything that creeps on the earth, in which there is life, I have given every green herb for food."

It might tickle your funny bone to think of a *Tyrannosaurus rex* tearing into shrubs, fruits, and vegetables with those ferocious fangs, but pandas have sharp teeth, too, and they eat an almost completely vegetarian diet.

After Adam sinned, death entered the scene, and everything turned upside down. Dinosaurs like *T. rex*, *Spinosaurus*, and *Allosaurus* turned into Meat Lovers. *T. rex* teeth and teeth marks found on other dino fossils offer clues that they fought and ate each other.

Other dinosaurs stuck with Team Veggie, and some of their super snacks still exist today—grass, rice, ferns, rotting wood, magnolias, and sago palms. Yum! Terrific treats for a "terribly great lizard."

Where Dinosaurs Lived

Dinosaurs probably lived in swampy places. We find them buried with many other swamp creatures like beavers, salamanders, crocodiles, turtles, and frogs. Some dinos also lived on higher ground near rivers.

Evolutionists used to think dinos lived before grass and flowering plants evolved. But now they know better. We find modern plants like oaks, orchids, magnolias, and grasses buried with dinosaurs or even fossilized in their bellies. If evolution scientists believed God's Word in Genesis, they would have already known dinosaurs lived among some grass and flowering plants.

The Bible mentions a dinosaur-like creature called behemoth that lived after the Flood. In the book of Job, God describes the behemoth's living conditions like this:

> "He lies under the lotus trees, in a covert of reeds and marsh. The lotus trees cover him with their shade; the willows by the brook surround him." (Job 40:21-22)

Doesn't that sound just like a swamp? Home sweet swampy home!

Dino Diseases

Did dinosaurs get sick or hurt like we do?

Yes, fossils reveal that dinos suffered from injuries and disease. One *T. rex* fossil had cancer. We can tell by the fossilized bone tumor on its spine. That same dino also had tooth marks on top of his skull showing that another *T. rex* attacked him. (What a terrible day he was having!)

Other fossils show signs of parasite infections and other unpleasant effects that came when sin and death entered God's perfectly created world.

At the end of this book, we'll talk about God's plan to get rid of all sickness and pain for good. One day, He's going to make things right again. Keep reading!

parasite

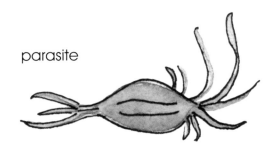

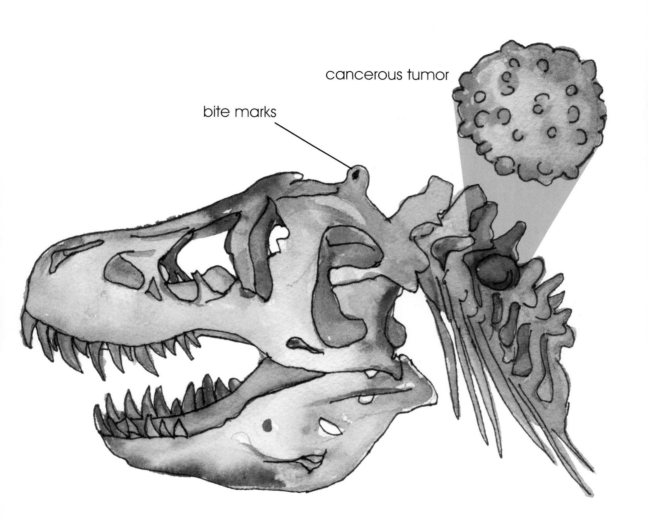

cancerous tumor

bite marks

A Dinosaur in the Bible?

Did you know the Bible may mention dinosaurs and other extinct reptiles? Sir Richard Owen invented the word "dinosaur" in 1841, long after the Bible was written. But the Bible uses names like dragon, serpent, and behemoth for huge, fierce creatures.

> "Look now at the behemoth, which I made along with you; he eats grass like an ox. See now, his strength is in his hips, and his power is in his stomach muscles. He moves his tail like a cedar; the sinews of his thighs are tightly knit. His bones are like beams of bronze, his ribs like bars of iron." (Job 40:15-18)

These verses describe a creature that sounds just like a Long-Neck Dino! Long-Necks like *Brachiosaurus* ate plants—including grass. They had a unique hip design, and when they walked their tails swayed like a cedar tree swaying in the wind.

When God told Job to look at behemoth, he may have turned to see a real-life, in-the-flesh, stomping, crunching, munching dinosaur—a creature we only see as bare bones today!

Dinos and the Flood

Around 4,000 years ago, the earth became filled with evil and violence. Can you imagine how terrible a place it must have been?

God judged the whole world with a global flood. But He knew one man in the middle of the chaos who still honored Him: Noah. He gave Noah the building plans for an enormous box called an Ark. It was like a big boat. The Ark gave Noah, his family, and some of every kind of air-breathing, land-living animal an escape from the coming disaster.

Dinosaurs lived on land and breathed air, so of course they boarded the Ark, too! After God shut the door, the fountains of the earth broke open—water came up from the ground! It also came from the skies. It rained for 40 days and 40 nights. The water rose, volcanoes erupted, and the continents split.

After a year, the Flood's waters had drained off and the ground dried. Noah, his family, and all the animals

stepped out
of the Ark to find
a very different
world. They were the
only ones left.

Every person and land
animal that didn't make
it on the Ark died. How
sad! And many of those
creatures turned into the
fossils we see in museums
today.

But that's not the end
of the dino story. You're
probably wondering…what
happened to the ones
that survived on the Ark?

Answers for Noah's Ark

How big was Noah's Ark?

The Ark measured 450 feet long. That's longer than a football field! Plus, it had three decks going up! The boat could hold about 14,000 tons of cargo, including 125,000 sheep-size animals.

How many dinosaurs boarded the Ark?

In Genesis 6:20, God told Noah, "Of the birds after their kind, of animals after their kind, and of every creeping thing of the earth after its kind, two of every kind will come to you to keep them alive."

There were about 60 dinosaur families, so that's probably how many different types of dinos boarded the Ark. Two of each would equal 120 dinos.

How could the gigantic dinos fit?

Noah didn't have to take grown-up dinosaurs

on the Ark. God probably brought young dinos since they were smaller.

What did the dinosaurs eat?

While on board, the dinosaurs could have survived as vegetarians. They ate only plants before the Fall, so they didn't necessarily have to eat other animals to live.

What if I have more questions?

The best thing you can do when you have questions is to seek good, solid answers. The Institute for Creation Research has much more information on dinosaurs, the Flood, the Ark, and more! Check out our website (ICR.org) to find out how God's Word can be trusted even in the details.

Where Did All the Dinos Go?

What happened to our dino friends after they stomped, scuttled, and trotted off the Ark? They spread out over the globe and multiplied—and so did all the other surviving creatures.

The Flood turned the world topsy-turvy. Some of Earth's water froze into thick sheets of ice that stretched across continents. This caused a global Ice Age that lasted for hundreds of years. With less liquid water, the sea level dropped and exposed dry land between some continents. Animals crossed these land bridges to live and thrive in new places.

After the ice melted, many dinosaur habitats

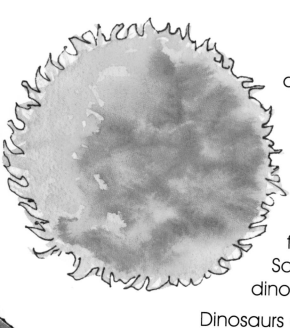

disappeared. The dinos that survived found a few warm places to live. But people competed for those places and probably felt threatened by such large (and sometimes ferocious) animals. So, they hunted the dinosaurs.

Dinosaurs appear to have gone extinct. But within the last century, some people claimed they spotted dinosaur-like creatures living in isolated places, such as deep swamps and thick forests. Is it possible that a few dinosaur kinds still exist somewhere in the world today?

Flood Fossils

When animals die, they are usually eaten by bacteria or other animals (yuck!). They can only turn into fossils if mud quickly buries them. This could happen during a massive flood or mudslide.

Thousands of years ago, Noah's Flood covered the whole earth with water and deep layers of mud. Every land creature that didn't get on the Ark drowned and was buried. So, even though fossils form under rare conditions, it makes sense that we find so many millions of them in the earth today.

Fossil graveyards contain lots of animals buried together in groups. Ocean animals are often mixed with land animals, including dinosaurs. How could animals living on land and others living in water wind up buried in the same place upon dry land today? A flood that covered the earth offers the best answer.

- The dino fossil on page 35 is known as *Compsognathus*.
- Fossils of long-neck creatures from all over the world have similar, extremely bent postures.
- This matches what long-neck animals look like after they choke on mud.

Living Fossils

Can the kinds of fossilized creatures we see in museums still be living somewhere today?

If you said yes, you're right! Sometimes animals or plants that evolution scientists thought were extinct for millions of years show up alive. These are called living fossils. One famous example is the coelacanth (SEE-luh-kanth), a fishy name you don't want to catch in a spelling bee!

Evolutionists said the coelacanth evolved from fish and later turned into an amphibian. It supposedly died out around 70 million years ago. But in 1938, one was captured off the coast of South Africa!

If evolution is true, why hasn't the coelacanth changed in over 70 million years? Lots of other living fossils—magnolia flowers, gar fish, and lobsters—have been found with very few changes, too. Answer: They didn't evolve—God created these fascinating animals and plants just a few thousand years ago.

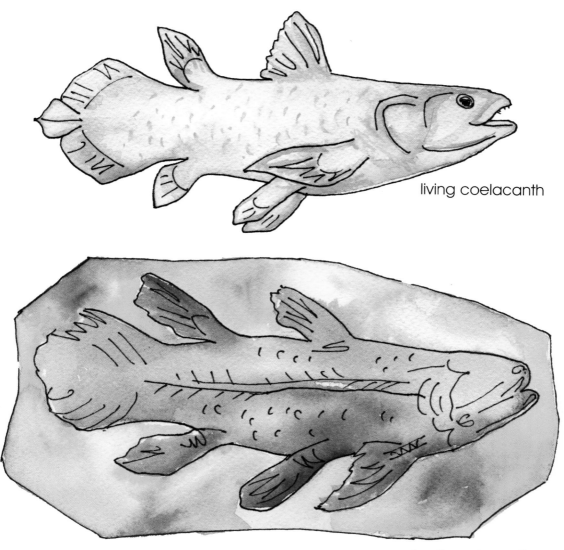

living coelacanth

fossil coelacanth

Five Ways Fossils Form

Did you know that fossils almost never form today? Dead plants and animals usually rot or animals eat them. They only turn into fossils if they are buried quickly by mud. Check out five forms of fossils.

Mineralized Fossils

A mineralized fossil is a plant or animal that has turned to stone. Water washes dinosaur body parts away and replaces them with minerals. The minerals create exact copies of the creature for us to study.

Preserved Fossils

Preserved fossils aren't just copies or imprints—they actually contain original parts of the dinosaur! They have original soft tissue such as skin, muscle, and blood cells in them. Scientists found blood vessels in the leg bone of a *T. rex* and a Duck-Bill Dino…and the blood was still red!

Carbonized Fossils

Carbonized fossils typically form from plants. But when buried dinosaurs get hot underground, their tissues can leave behind a thin, black carbon layer.

Molds and Casts

Molds and casts show the shapes of dinosaur parts imprinted in rock. It's like pressing your hand onto play dough and seeing your fingerprints in it. A mold fossil of dinosaur skin shows the beautiful texture and pattern of the scales.

Trace Fossils

Anything dinosaurs left behind is a trace fossil. Some of the coolest include dinosaur tracks or animal burrows, but trace fossils can also be dinosaur droppings. Watch where you step!

Eyewitness at the Start

How do you know how old you are? Did a scientist figure out your age using a natural process like tooth wear? Or the wrinkling of your face? Or the grayness of your hair? Those clues may help them make a good guess, but your age would be much more accurate if an eyewitness could tell you when you were born.

Your eyewitness could be your mom or dad. Or you could look at a birth certificate. Wouldn't it be nice if an eyewitness recorded the birth of Earth?

He actually did!

Our great Creator is the most reliable eyewitness imaginable. He helped men write Genesis, which describes the birth of Earth. The biblical timeline shows us that this happened only thousands of years ago, not millions. And Genesis never says anything about evolution.

Scientists look to natural processes like the forming of rock layers, land erosion, or decaying carbon to guess the age of the earth and how it came to be. But an honest eyewitness, like the God who was there from the beginning, provides a much more trustworthy perspective.

How Old Are Dino Fossils?

How old are dinosaur fossils? Well, no one's lived long enough to count all their birthdays. But according to the Bible, they couldn't be more than thousands of years old.

Many scientists say dino fossils formed in layers of rock tens of millions of years ago, not thousands. (They'd need a whole lot more candles for that Jurassic cake!)

Who's right—those guys? Or scientists who believe the Bible?

Let's use an old-fashioned clock called an hourglass to understand some limits in guessing time.

In an hourglass, all the sand grains slip from the top to the bottom in an hour. We can measure how fast they flow and the amounts in each chamber.

If we came upon an hourglass, could we figure out how long it has been running? Only if we knew for sure that:

- All the sand started in the upper chamber.

- The sand fell without stopping.

- No sand was added or escaped from the hourglass.

But we can't know for sure that all of those things are true if we didn't watch it the whole time. Something may have tipped the hourglass on its side. Sand could enter or leave through an unexpected hole. If any of these things happened when we weren't looking, it would trick us into calculating the wrong amount of time.

In a similar way, no one knows for sure if scientists' assumptions about the rocks and fossils are true—they weren't watching them form over millions of years. But many still use these rock-age guesses to say the Bible is wrong and the world is millions of years old.

They might not know of the awesome evidence that shows fossil rocks are only thousands of years old, just like the Bible says.

Rock Layers Report Noah's Flood

Wanna take a road trip? Hop in the van! Instead of arguing with your little brother in the backseat, grab your binoculars and look out the window. We're about to drive through a road in the hills, so pay attention to the rocky walls on both sides. The roads cut through mountain passes allow us to see many layers of rock.

Notice how the lower rock layers look very different from the top soil layer? If you take a closer peek, you'll see the top soil layer contains roots, worm tunnels, and uneven surfaces. You'll often find ruts and gullies from many years of erosion. ("Erosion" describes how rain washes sand and soil down rivers and into oceans.)

But deeper rock layers usually have almost perfectly flat surfaces. If millions of years passed between each layer, then shouldn't the upper surface of each one have millions of years' worth of ruts and gullies, plus plant roots and animal tunnels?

Well, most of them don't.

The deep rock layers that contain dinosaur fossils are mostly flat and smooth. They are very tightly packed against the layers above and below them. This shows that all the layers—the whole stack of rock pancakes—flowed into place one right after another.

And Bible clues tell us why.

Noah's Flood laid down thousands of feet of these layers of sand and mud, at times mixing them with dinosaurs and other animals—all in one year! That left no time for erosion to carve ruts or gullies between layers.

Now put away your binoculars, pat yourself on the back, and enjoy the rest of the trip.

Thinking in a Circle

"Circular reasoning" means using the very thing you're trying to prove as evidence of its truth.

Secular scientists use circular reasoning when they assign ages to fossils. They assume a dinosaur fossil's age before they try to determine its age. Their thinking goes like this:

"We believe this dinosaur's age to be about 188 million years because it's buried in a rock layer deposited about 188 million years ago. And we know this rock layer is 188 million years old. Why? Because this dino was found buried with other fossils dated at 188 million years old."

Using circular thinking, evolution scientists assume that millions of years of evolution happened and then use that to guess millions of years of age for a dinosaur. Then they guess the age of rock layers based on the guessed ages of the fossils buried within them.

This leads evolution scientists to misinterpret and even ignore evidence that shows dino and rock layer dates of only thousands of years.

Age of the Fossil

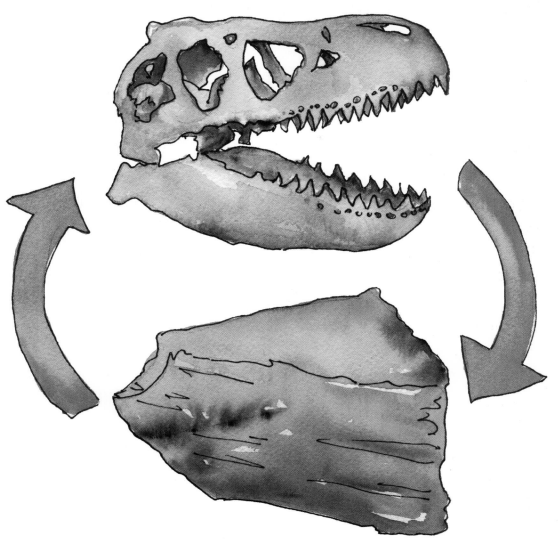

Age of the Rock

Radiocarbon in Dino Bones

Elements are building blocks that make up everything. Carbon is one of those building blocks, and it's in every living thing on Earth—even you! A tiny fraction of carbon called radiocarbon is radioactive.

wood

When living things die, the radiocarbon inside them decays. Tests show that something older than 100,000 years shouldn't have any radiocarbon left at all. If dinosaurs lived millions of years ago as evolution scientists say, then why do their bones still have radiocarbon in them?

Evolutionists dated a Duck-Bill Dino bone found in South Dakota at about 68 million years old. But when it was sent to a lab for carbon-dating tests, it returned with an age of only thousands of years. With radiocarbon still inside, this bone— and the dinosaur it belonged to—has to be younger than 100,000 years.

coal

Carbon also showed up inside a *Triceratops* fossil from Montana, as well as in fossils, wood, coal, oil, and diamonds from all over the world and throughout various rock layers.

Finding radiocarbon in dino bones is a big problem for an evolutionist, but it's a fantastic find if you believe God created the world only thousands of years ago, just as the Bible says.

Triceratops skull

49

Soft Stuff in Hard Rocks

Have you ever seen a dead bug on the sidewalk? It can be a pretty gross sight with ants crawling all over it and eating the soft parts of its body. Yuck! Most likely, very little of it will be left there next month, let alone next year.

Well, dead dinosaurs are kind of like that, too. Their bodies decay quickly. Even when preserved in rock, soft parts like skin, blood cells, bone parts, and DNA can only last a few thousand years before they break down.

But scientists have discovered red blood cell remnants in mosasaurs, theropods, hadrosaurs, and others. They also found probable dinosaur DNA, which decays even quicker than blood cells!

If dinosaurs were millions of years old as evolutionists say, this soft stuff should be long gone.

Some scientists claim that iron in the dinosaurs' blood preserves soft tissues for millions of years. But experiments only show iron preserving soft tissues for several years, and only under conditions that do not match fossil environments.

Soft tissue discoveries show dinosaur fossils are only thousands of years old, not millions.

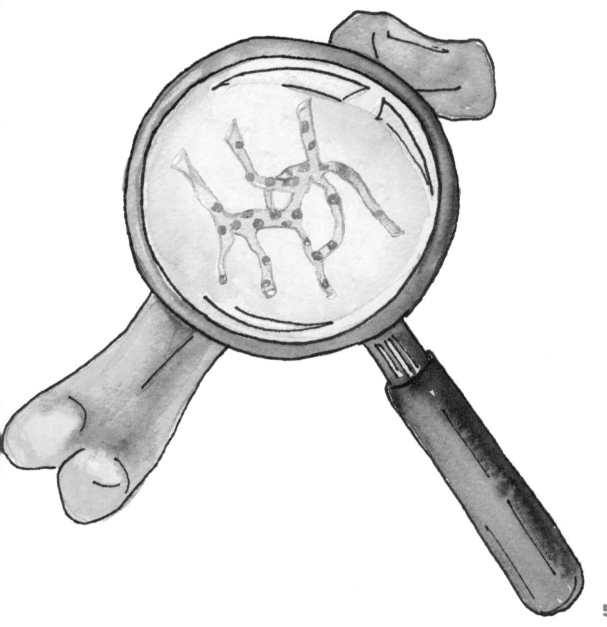

Dino Camo

God designed some creatures with camouflage coloring that helps them blend in with their surroundings. Polar bears' fur matches their snowy homes, and green caterpillars hide out easily while they munch on plants. Animals that live in forests have darker shading along their backs and down their sides to help them take cover in the shady woods. This game of hide and seek keeps predators from spotting them easily.

A well-preserved Chinese *Psittacosaurus* fossil has some of its original skin, though it's dried up like a mummy. Amazingly, it displays a typical forest-living shade pattern. Its scaly skin is darker down its back and sides.

What made this discovery possible? The dino has dark-colored chemicals stored in its skin. And its scales made of keratin—the same material as our fingernails—are still there.

Skin can last thousands of years. But skin can't last a million years before decaying. If this *Psittacosaurus* skin was deposited only thousands of years ago in Noah's Flood, then no wonder its skin still has original scales and camouflage shading!

Dinosaur Eggs

Which came first, the *Psittacosaurus* or the egg?

Eggs aren't just for chickens, you know! Reptiles lay eggs, too. Scientists look at preserved egg embryos (dino babies still developing in the egg) to find out which dinosaur laid the eggs. The biggest ones come from the Long-Neck Dinos—they laid eggs as large as footballs.

Normally, reptiles hide their eggs under plants or in crevices to keep them safe. But some dinosaurs seemed to lay their eggs out in open fields. This doesn't fit with normal reptile behavior. These eggs were buried during Noah's Flood.

As the water washed onto land, dinosaurs didn't have time to hide their eggs. They laid them wherever they could during their rush to higher ground.

Some fossilized dino eggs still have vibrant colors. But how can that be? Colors fade quickly, so these eggs couldn't have been buried more than thousands of years ago. And since they must be buried quickly to form a fossil, the Flood makes a great explanation for still-colorful, well-preserved dino eggs.

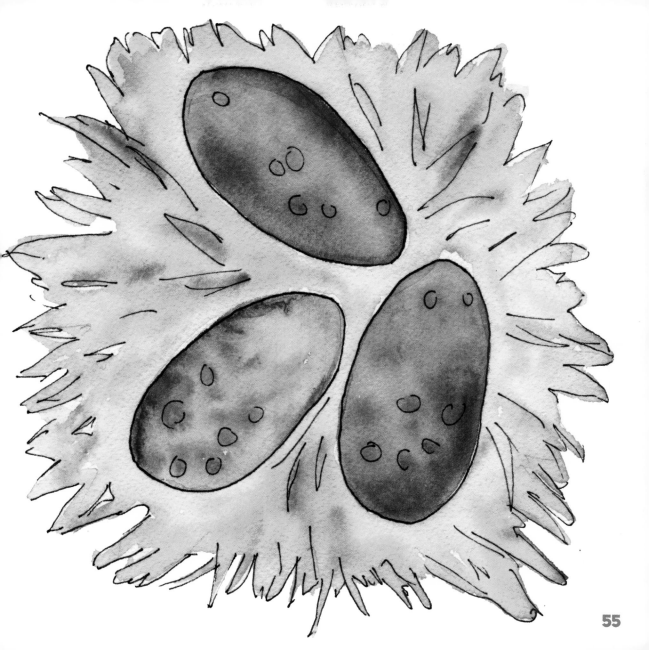

The Truth about Birds and Dinos

Did dinosaurs evolve into birds by changing in small ways over a long period of time? Evolutionists think so. But the fossils we find are either birds or dinosaurs. When one scientist claims to have found a fossil with both dinosaur and bird parts, other scientists always disagree. So, there are no undisputed part-bird, part-dinosaur fossils.

Dinosaurs and birds are also found buried in the same rock layers. This shows that they lived at the same time. One did not exist long before the other.

What would have to change for a dinosaur to turn into a bird?

- **Hip structure.** Evolutionists say that Sharp-Tooth Dinos evolved into birds, but they have hips like a lizard, not a bird.

- **Breathing system.** Bird lungs allow air to pass right through them. This supports flight. But dinosaurs had lungs like other reptiles and mammals. These lungs fill and expand, then empty and shrink.

- **Flight design.** To fly, a bird needs fully formed

connecting feathers and lightweight, hollow bones. An undisputed dinosaur with feathers has never been discovered. And *T. rex* couldn't fly because his tailbone would be too heavy!

If a dinosaur changed into a bird over time, it would not survive. The animal would die while waiting to develop a fully formed breathing system, working hips, or the ability to fly. Dino-to-bird evolution isn't just a tall tale. It's absolutely impossible!

Dino Art and Artifacts

The word "dinosaur" was only invented within the last couple of centuries. But stories and artwork of dragons have been around much longer than that. Were dragons actually dinosaurs?

Around 800 years ago, people carved animals into the walls of a temple in Cambodia. Some of them look like pigs, lizards, and monkeys. But one of the carvings looks just like a *Stegosaurus*! If no one knew about dinosaur fossils back then, how could they know what a *Stegosaurus* looked like? They had to see one in real life.

A piece of fabric hanging in a French castle shows a creature that looks like one of the Duck-Bill Dinos. And a cathedral in England has carvings of Long-Neck Dinos in its floor.

Marco Polo, the well-known explorer, wrote about his experience with huge "serpents" that had two short legs, claws, and big jaws. These mysterious beasts sound an awful lot like dinosaurs!

With all of this evidence and more, it's easy to believe that dinosaurs and people lived on Earth at the very same time both before and after the Flood.

- This Native American rock art was found in a Peruvian jungle.
- The human figures surround a creature that looks like a Long-Neck Dino.

The Sharp-Tooth Dinos

The Sharp-Tooth Dinos—officially known as Theropoda—were fast and fierce. They include dinosaurs like the famous *T. rex* and *Velociraptor*. As Meat Lovers, they hunted with powerful legs and jaws.

God designed most of their bones to be hollow. This made their skeletons lighter for speedy racing and chasing. The many joints in their skulls

and necks gave them great flexibility when biting and chewing.

Evolutionists believe that these dinosaurs later evolved into birds. But members of the Sharp-Tooth Dinos didn't have beaks, and their hips were like a lizard, not a bird!

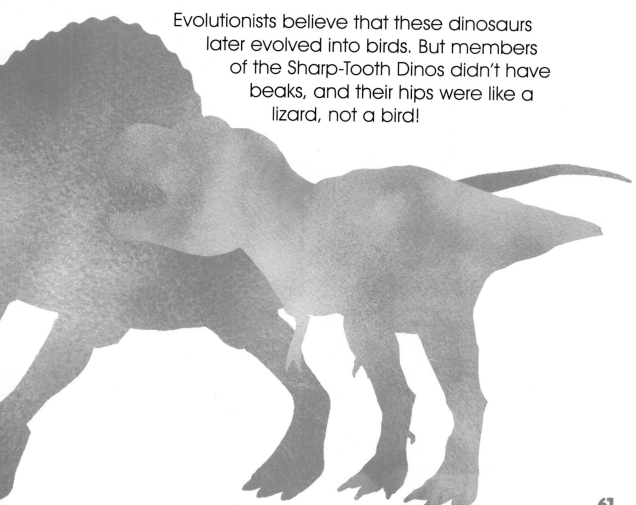

Tyrannosaurus rex

Meat Lovers

- *A celebrity dino with a huge body, small forearms, and ferocious grin.*
- *Its jaws crushed prey with the same force as an elephant sitting on a person.*
- *Sue, the largest known* T. rex *fossil, stands over 12 feet tall and measures over 40 feet long.*

Big hello to all my fans out there! I'm pretty famous, so you've probably heard about me. My best friends call me *T. rex*. I've certainly left my mark—my tooth marks have been found on other dinosaurs.

Evolutionists like to say that my brain is like a bird's, but my brain is shaped much more like a reptile's. My intelligence, way of thinking, and senses are similar to an alligator's.

Thanks to my huge nostrils and the large part of my brain made for smelling, it's easy to sniff out when dinner's ready—even if it's miles away! Many dinos have eyes on either side of their head, but mine are set so I can look straight ahead. All the better to see you with, my dear! CHOMP!

Fun Facts
Discovered: 1900 (Montana)
Pronunciation: tye-RAN-uh-SAWR-us rex
Name means: Tyrant lizard king
Rock system: Upper Cretaceous
Size: 12 ft. tall, 42 ft. long, 6 tons
Dinosaur classification: Theropoda

63

Velociraptor

Meat Lovers

- *A turkey-size dino with a shark smile and a big toe you don't want to step on!*
- *Two enlarged claws on its hind feet may have been used to grasp prey.*
- *Often mistaken for a movie star.*

As my name suggests, I'm a quick little thief. I can run up to 24 miles per hour. That's faster than most of you humans! My chompers curve backward—similar to a shark's—and boy are they sharp! These toothy tools slash at prey, making sure there's no escape. Bwahaha!

I'm a certified bone cruncher. Researchers once found a three-inch piece of pterosaur bone fossilized in my ribcage. Noah's Flood probably buried me at lightning speed— I didn't even have time to digest my lunch!

You might think you've seen me before. I get that a lot! Everyone thinks I acted in the movie *Jurassic Park*, but that was actually my friend *Deinonychus*. They called him *Velociraptor*, but he's bigger than me and has never once turned a doorknob!

Fun Facts
Discovered: 1923 (Mongolia)
Pronunciation: veh-LOSS-ih-RAP-tor
Name means: Rapid robber
Rock system: Upper Cretaceous
Size: 2.5 ft. tall, 6 ft. long, 35 lbs.
Dinosaur classification: Theropoda

Allosaurus

Meat Lovers

- *Sometimes called the "land shark."*
- *Sliced and diced with nearly 70 tiny saber-sword teeth.*
- *Claws measured up to eight inches.*

Come closer. I don't bite…

Well, maybe I do. Scientists found a *Stegosaurus* with my teeth marks in it. Oops, sorry Steggie! In my defense, he started it. And I have wounds from his tail spikes to prove it!

My giant jaws may remind you of a slippery shark, but these tiny, razor-sharp teeth did all their slashing on land. That is, until Noah's Flood covered the earth. The Flood buried me and turned me into a fossil along with many of my friends!

My *Allosaurus* pal "Big Al" was fossilized in the worldwide Flood, too. Someone found him in Wyoming. He had cracked ribs and vertebrae—all that rushing water is no joke! Scientists took him to the University of Wyoming Geological Museum, and you can still see him there today. Pay him a visit sometime!

Fun Facts
Discovered: 1869 (Colorado)
Pronunciation: AL-uh-SAWR-us
Name means: Different lizard
Rock system: Upper Jurassic
Size: 12 ft. tall, 30 ft. long, 2 tons
Dinosaur classification:
Theropoda

Spinosaurus

Meat Lovers

- *The largest meat-eating dino, with a built-in sail and a crocodile smile.*
- *Could walk on two legs or all four.*
- *No complete skeleton has ever been found.*

Ahoy, mates!

You'll know I'm sailing your way when you see the webbed spine on my back cutting through the river. We spinosaurs spent most of our time in water, but we had land legs, too! Our fossils were found in Egypt and Morocco.

Some creation scientists think the Bible talks about me when it uses the name "leviathan." Leviathan was a beast that left marks in the mud and a white wake as he swam through water.

World War II bombing destroyed the original and most complete *Spinosaurus* fossil in a German museum. But more recent fossil finds are giving scientists a better understanding of my spectacular design.

Fun Facts
Discovered: 1912 (Egypt)
Pronunciation: SPY-nuh-SAWR-us
Name means: Spine lizard
Rock system: Upper Cretaceous
Size: 14 ft. tall, 50 ft. long, 7 tons
Dinosaur classification:
Theropoda

The Long-Neck Dinos

The Long-Neck Dinos—also known as Sauropodomorpha—included the biggest dinosaurs. Some of them weighed as much as two school buses! They walked on four legs, ate plants, and, as you might guess, had super-long necks. Their fossils are often found in Flood rocks from the Jurassic system.

God designed Long-Necks with lizard-like hips, small heads, and arched hip bones. Their long necks with weight-saving neck and tail bones and lightweight heads let them reach high into trees for food. The arched hip bones helped to support the weight of their body. God knew exactly what they needed!

Diplodocus

Team Veggie

- *A slender, lanky Long-Neck Dino with a whip of a tail.*
- *One of the first and longest dinos put on public display.*
- *Its tail has about 80 vertebrae!*

My name may twist your tongue, so you can call me Dippy for short. *Diplodocus* means double beam—an ideal name since two rods make a "V" shape along the underside of my tail. Speaking of tails, mine thins out at the end like a smart little whip. Scientists think I used it to warn the rest of my herd: Stranger danger! Snap, crackle, pop!

God designed me with the perfect tools for munching! My peg-shape teeth devour soft plants and strip yummy leaves and needles from branches. After I swallow, gastroliths in my gizzard (stomach stones in a muscle pocket) help me finish digesting these tasty treats.

Many fossils in my family are found with the skull separated from the body—but don't lose your head over it! Headless dino fossils show the Flood's waters packed a powerful punch!

Fun Facts
Discovered: 1877 (Colorado)
Pronunciation: dih-PLOD-uh-kus
Name means: Double beam
Rock system: Upper Jurassic
Size: 30 ft. tall, 89 ft. long, 14 tons
Dinosaur classification:
    Sauropodomorpha

Apatosaurus

Team Veggie

- *A Long-Neck Dino with two names.*
- *Depicted on a U.S. stamp in 1989 as Brontosaurus.*
- *One of the largest beasts to ever walk the earth.*

Welcome to the circus—my 20-foot-long neck and 30-foot tail create quite the balancing act! My tail can crack like a whip, and the sound is louder than a cannon exploding.

My real name is *Apatosaurus*, but you can call me TheDinoFormerlyKnownAs*Brontosaurus* for short. Othniel C. Marsh named my bones *Apatosaurus* in 1877. When he found a bigger Long-Neck Dino fossil, he called it *Brontosaurus* because it looked different. Turns out, we're both the same dinosaur!

The Flood's waters overtook all of the poor creatures that didn't make it on the Ark. My brother Einstein was one of them, and you can visit his exhibit in Monterrey, Mexico. Tell him I sent you…and be sure to call him by the right name!

Fun Facts

Discovered: 1877 (Colorado)
Pronunciation: ah-PAT-uh-SAWR-us
Name means: Deceptive lizard
Rock system: Upper Jurassic
Size: 30 ft. tall, 75 ft. long, 33 tons
Dinosaur classification: Sauropodomorpha

Argentinosaurus

Team Veggie

- *A Long-Neck Dino weighing as much as 10 elephants!*
- *The largest known dinosaur.*
- *Discovered by an Argentine farmer.*

Hola! My name is *Argentinosaurus*. Can you guess what South American country I was discovered in?

No one has found a complete *Argentinosaurus* skeleton, but my fossil thigh bone is taller than the average man. Comparing that bone to other dinosaur bones, scientists guessed how big the rest of my body was: ¡muy grande!

As the largest known dino, I only traveled at about five miles per hour—the same speed as a fast-walking hombre.

My arched backbone was perfectly designed. It distributed weight evenly to my giant legs. And my backbone and legs worked with my specially designed neck and tail muscles so I could easily raise my head to eat.

Great design in a giant like me didn't come by accident. Design always comes from a designer. Who do you think designed me? ¡Un Creador maravilloso!

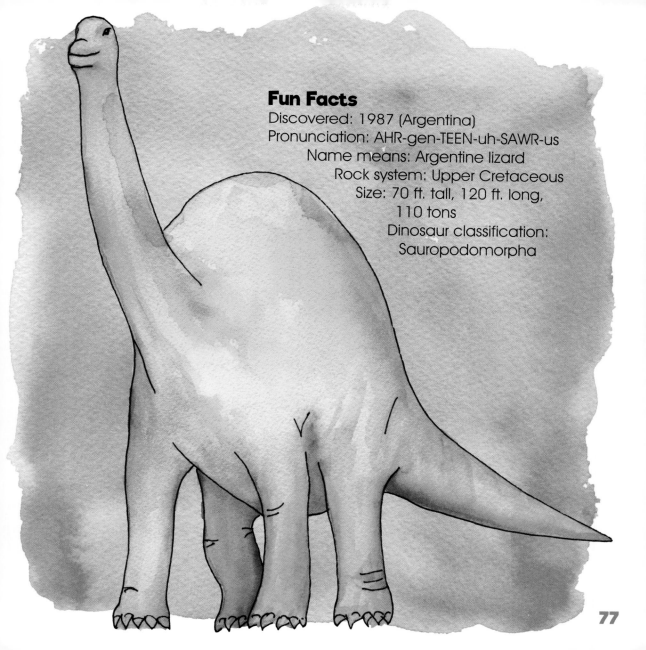

Fun Facts

Discovered: 1987 (Argentina)
Pronunciation: AHR-gen-TEEN-uh-SAWR-us
Name means: Argentine lizard
Rock system: Upper Cretaceous
Size: 70 ft. tall, 120 ft. long,
110 tons
Dinosaur classification:
Sauropodomorpha

Brachiosaurus

Team Veggie

- *A Long-Neck Dino with a bumpy nose and a giraffe-shape body.*
- *The front legs stood taller than the back legs.*
- *Its head may have reached up to 60 ft. above the ground.*

Is that a gigantic giraffe in the distance? No, wait…it's me, *Brachiosaurus*! My long neck and front legs may remind you of those super-tall creatures at the zoo, but I'm much bigger than any animal you've ever seen.

I lived in North America, but a fossil of my cousin *Giraffatitan brancai* was found in Africa. Why were two dinos in the same family found an ocean apart? It's likely that the continents were one big land mass and they later divided during Noah's Flood.

G. brancai has different bone sizes from mine, but creation scientists say we're both brachiosaurs. We're just displaying the super cool variety God created within our kind.

Fun Facts
Discovered: 1900 (Colorado)
Pronunciation: BRACK-ee-uh-SAWR-us
Name means: Arm lizard
Rock system: Upper Jurassic
Size: 50 ft. tall, 100 ft. long, 60 tons
Dinosaur classification: Sauropodomorpha

The Helmet Dinos

Can you say Marginocephalia three times fast? How about we call this group the Helmet Dinos instead!

The Helmet Dinos can be divided into two groups: Horn Heads and Dome Heads.

Horn Heads like *Triceratops* measured 20 to 30 feet long. They showed off their horns and frills and had a powerful bite. Ouch!

Dome Heads like *Pachycephalosaurus* had skullcaps up to 10 inches thick. Around six to seven feet tall, they weighed about 900 pounds. Dome Heads usually walked on two feet and ate plants. Their tails stuck straight out behind them, and they were tough to beat in a footrace!

Triceratops

Team Veggie

- *An army tank of a dino with three horns and a frill.*
- *About the size of an elephant.*
- *Charged up to 10-20 miles per hour.*

At-ten-tion! Sergeant *Triceratops* is my name and scuffling with *T. rex* is my game. *Triceratops* means "three-horned face," which should be no surprise. I displayed a small horn on the tip of my nose and two large ones above my eyes.

I had a big, bony neck frill and a threatening stance. You might find me a little intimidating, but don't sweat it—I only ate plants.

A *Triceratops* and *T. rex* became fossils in the middle of a fight. My brother received a terrible bite! Sharp tyrannosaur teeth got stuck in his skull. "Ouch, that hurts!" he howled.

My cousins had different patterns of horns and frills. But we're all part of the same family. We're tough but chill. The same goes for *Torosaurus*—scientists used to think he was new. He had a larger frill and horns, but the differences were few. Now they think *Torosaurus* was just my Pops, a bigger and braver veteran *Triceratops*.

Fun Facts
Discovered: 1887 (Colorado)
Pronunciation: try-SAIR-uh-tops
Name means: Three-horned face
Rock system: Upper Cretaceous
Size: 9.5 ft. tall, 26 ft. long, 7 tons
Dinosaur classification:
Marginocephalia

Protoceratops

Team Veggie

- *Looks like a Triceratops with fewer horns.*
- *Known as the "sheep" of the dinosaurs.*
- *Discovered by the real Indiana Jones.*

I'm *Protoceratops*, known as the "sheep" of the dinosaurs, but it's not too baa-aad.

As an expert landscaper, my beak trims tough plants, and my back teeth grind them up like compost.

I don't make a big fuss, but I do have one claim to fame. I was discovered by a famous scientist and adventurer, Roy Chapman Andrews, in 1922. His daring explorations for ancient artifacts inspired the movie character Indiana Jones.

Fossils form fast. My brother in China bit a *Velociraptor* in the arm, and they became fossils in the middle of their fight. His mouth is still locked on that Sharp-Tooth Dino to this very day! Could it have been Noah's Flood that buried them in the middle of their battle?

Fun Facts
Discovered: 1922 (Mongolia)
Pronunciation: pro-toe-SAIR-uh-tops
Name means: First horned face
Rock system: Upper Cretaceous
Size: 2.6 ft. tall, 6 ft. long, 400 lbs.
Dinosaur classification: Marginocephalia

Psittacosaurus

Team Veggie

- *A waist-high dino with a strong, sharp beak and a finned tail.*
- *Fossils found in Thailand, Asia, China, and Mongolia.*
- *A creature that looks like a Tasmanian devil was found with a* Psittacosaurus *fossilized inside its belly!*

Hey dude, I'm *Psittacosaurus*! I've got a fin, but I'm no fish. I've got a beak, but I'm no parrot.

I walked on all fours as a tiny tot, but now I move on two powerful hind legs. My flexible tail makes scientists wonder if I could swim, too! Did I swing it side to side through the water like a crocodile? Maybe. A water-logged life would explain the fin-like fibers on my tail.

Over 400 fossils of my dino family have been found, and they range from seven-foot adults to six-inch babies. Thirty-two of those *Psittacosaurus* babies were fossilized in China. Some blame volcanoes and mudflows for burying them. Creation scientists think the volcanoes erupted and mud flowed during Noah's Flood. The floodwaters overwhelmed the nest before they could leave home. So sad!

Fun Facts

Discovered: 1923 (Mongolia)
Pronunciation: sit-TACK-co-sawr-us
Name means: Parrot lizard
Rock system: Lower Cretaceous
Size: 3.5 ft. tall, 6.5 ft. long, 50 lbs.
Dinosaur classification: Marginocephalia

Pachycephalosaurus

Team Veggie

- *A walking Dome Head who's ready to rumble.*
- *Stood about as tall as a man.*
- *Ate fruits and seeds with its small, leaf-shape teeth.*

I can be a little "boneheaded" sometimes, but I'm always ready to rumble. My 10-inch-thick skull keeps me prepared for action!

Back in the day, I fed on low-lying shrubs and ran in herds with my buddies. Some scientists think we may have butted heads like bighorn rams to fight over who would be the leader. A scan of my fossilized skull revealed scars from lots of head injuries. But others think my neck bones may not be strong enough to survive such hard collisions. So, my bone dome stays a mystery.

Other scientists think we fought like giraffes, knocking each other with the sides of our heads. My five-inch spikes would definitely do some damage.

Few known body skeletons of my family exist, but fossilized pachycephalosaur skulls were discovered in Montana, South Dakota, and Wyoming. I guess we like to stay a-HEAD of the game. Hee-hee-hee!

Fun Facts
Discovered: 1860 (Montana)
Pronunciation: pak-ee-SEF-uh-lo-SAWR-us
Name means: Thick-headed lizard
Rock system: Upper Cretaceous
Size: 5-6 ft. tall, 15 ft. long, 900 lbs.
Dinosaur classification: Marginocephalia

The Armor Dinos

Introducing…the Armor Dinos! Also known as Thyreophora, these dinosaurs had bony plates on their bodies, and some had spiky tails. They ate plants, so they weren't dangerous—that is, as long as you stayed out of their way!

These dinos are divided into two main groups.

The first is the Fused Lizards, like *Ankylosaurus*. Bony plates covered their bodies as protective armor. And their huge clubbed tails could break the legs of a *T. rex*.

The second group is the Plated Lizards. Each had a row of bony plates on its back and a spiky tail. If you think that sounds like a

Stegosaurus, you're right. Stegosaurs were Plated Lizards. Fossils of the Armor Dinos are found mostly in Flood rocks from the Jurassic system.

Stegosaurus

Team Veggie

- *A popular four-leg dino with leaf-shape plates and a spiky tail.*
- *About the size of a bus.*
- *Ate low-lying shrubs with its peg-shape cheek teeth.*

My brain is about the size of an egg, but I'm smarter than they think! And what I don't have in brains I make up for in beauty.

My name means "roof lizard" because scientists thought my plates lay flat on my back like shingles on a roof. Now they realize these lovelies stood in an upright row or two down my neck and back.

Why do you think God designed stegosaurs with plates? Did they increase my good looks? Did they scare predators? Did they keep my body cool? No one knows for sure!

My portrait was carved on a Cambodian temple about a thousand years ago. I'm a great addition to any décor! But if no one knew about dinosaur bones back then, how did the Cambodians know what I looked like? They must have seen a stegosaur buddy living near them before stegosaurs went extinct.

Fun Facts

Discovered: 1876 (Colorado)
Pronunciation: STEG-uh-SAWR-us
Name means: Roof lizard
Rock system: Upper Jurassic
Size: 9-10 ft. tall, 30 ft. long, 3 tons
Dinosaur classification: Thyreophora

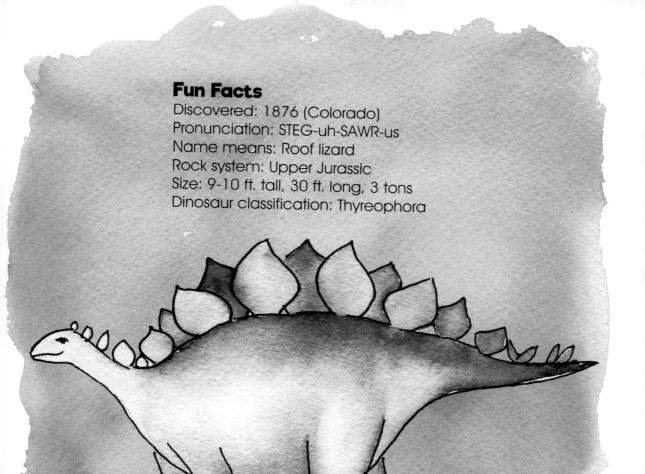

Ankylosaurus

Team Veggie

- *A stout, spiky dino covered in armor.*
- *Grazed on low-lying plants.*
- *Some had tail clubs strong enough to break predators' bones.*

With these short, stocky legs, I'm not the fastest runner. But why run when you're equipped to fight? In one fell swoop, I can swing my tail club and break the bones of any predator. Whack!

Plates of bone called osteoderms embedded in my skin make up this strong battle armor. My size and tough covering make me a less lovable prey for Meat Lovers.

A narrow beak works great for stripping leaves off low-lying shrubs. My leaf-shape teeth can chew, but they don't do much grinding. Scientists think I either stuck to the soft snacks or swallowed my meals in chunks.

My family's fossils come in some super cool shapes and sizes. My cousin *Sauropelta* had much longer spikes on his back and neck. And his tail had sharp, knife-like plates instead of a club. These design differences show God's creative plan for us all.

Fun Facts

Discovered: 1906 (Montana)
Pronunciation: ang-KIE-lo-SAWR-us
Name means: Fused lizard
Rock system: Upper Cretaceous
Size: 5.5 ft. tall, 20 ft. long, 5 tons
Dinosaur classification: Thyreophora

The Duck-Bill Dinos

The Duck-Bill Dinos ate plants and could walk on either two feet or all four. Officially known as Ornithopoda, their fossils are often found in Flood rocks from the Cretaceous system.

Duck-Bill Dino jaws were set a little lower than the cheek teeth. This is what gave their mouths a duck-bill look—

without the quacking. Their lack of armor and only medium height made them prime targets for more toothy tyrannosaurs.

One young member of this clan, Eddie the *Edmontosaurus*, hangs out at the Institute for Creation Research in Dallas, Texas.

Parasaurolophus

Team Veggie

- *A Duck-Bill Dino with a humpback and a musical head.*
- *Fossilized skin prints show small, rounded scales.*
- *A teen discovered a* Parasaurolophus *fossil in Utah!*

I don't mean to toot my own horn (wink, wink), but I was one of the largest land animals to run on two legs. I foraged for veggies on all fours, but when a predator came close I was off to a quick two-leg trot!

God gave me a mouth with a tooth factory. When my teeth wore out, new ones replaced them. At any given time, I had close to 800 teeth—and was always making more!

My five-foot-long crest connects to my nose and extends back over my shoulders. Inside the crest, tubes run from nostril to tip and back again. Blowing air through these tubes created a low foghorn sound.

Scientists used a fossilized *Parasaurolophus* skull to figure out my special horn call. Listen online to hear it for yourself!

Fun Facts

Discovered: 1920 (Alberta)
Pronunciation: par-ah-sawr-OL-uh-fus
Name means: Similar crested lizard
Rock system: Upper Cretaceous
Size: 10 ft. tall, 33 ft. long, 3 tons
Dinosaur classification: Ornithopoda

Iguanodon

Team Veggie

- *A narrow-headed dino with thumb spikes.*
- *Walked on two legs and on all fours.*
- *Could run about 15 miles per hour.*

Nice to meet you—I'm *Iguanodon*. You're looking at one of the earliest dinosaur kinds discovered. And I was the second to receive an official name.

It took scientists a while to understand what makes me, well...me. But they've come a long way since their early mistakes, and they're learning new things about dinos all the time!

In the beginning, they only had a few fossilized parts of an *Iguanodon* skeleton. So, scientists made a lot of guesses about how I looked. They first thought the spike on my thumb was a horn for my nose!

Thankfully, in 1878, two miners found 38 *Iguanodon* skeletons in a Belgian mine. They were probably buried together and fossilized during Noah's Flood. Having several complete models helped people see how *Iguanodons* are really designed. Studying how God put creatures together shows us how creative, powerful, and smart He is.

Fun Facts
Discovered: 1822 (England)
Pronunciation: ig-WAN-oh-don
Name means: Iguana-tooth
Rock system: Lower Cretaceous
Size: 12 ft. tall, 30 ft. long, 3 tons
Dinosaur classification: Ornithopoda

Brachylophosaurus

Team Veggie

- *A Duck-Bill Dino with a humpback and a bony crest down its spine.*
- *Hundreds of tiny stacked teeth shredded tough plants.*
- *One fossil leg bone still had blood vessels and dinosaur proteins inside!*

Hey, you guys, I'm Leonardo, a *Brachylophosaurus* from Montana. The Flood made me a mummy, but I'm not wrapped in cloths and stored in pyramids like Egyptian royalty. Sand filled in some of the spaces where my body once was, and then it hardened. This made a detailed sandy copy of some of my soft body parts.

My last meal is so well-preserved in my stomach that scientists can tell it was a gourmet delight of ferns, conifers, and magnolias. Oh, sweet memories!

One Brachy buddy still has original body material inside his fossil—not just sand. They found all kinds of proteins in his leg bone, including collagen and elastin.

Proteins can't last for even a million years before they turn into dust. How can they still rest inside my fellow fossil friend unless he's only thousands of years old?

Fun Facts

Discovered: 1936 (Canada)

Pronunciation:
brack-ee-LO-fuh-SAWR-us

Name means: Short-crested
lizard

Rock system: Upper Cretaceous

Size: 12 ft. tall, 28 ft. long,
3 tons

Dinosaur classification:
Ornithopoda

Dinosaurs Through Time

What a great time we've had talking about dinosaurs! We learned some fascinating dino facts and discovered that scientific evidence supports the Bible, not evolution. To help you remember the real dino story, let's review the facts just one more time.

Dinosaurs were…

CREATED to Be Friendly

God created dinosaurs on Day 6 of the creation week. This was the same day He created other land animals and humans. Dinosaurs were originally plant-eaters.

CORRUPTED into Carnivores

Adam and Eve sinned, bringing death into the world. Some dinosaurs became meat-eaters.

CARED for by Noah's Family

God flooded the world to punish evil. Noah's family and every creature on the Ark—including dinosaurs—survived.

CARRIED away in the Flood

Every land creature not on the Ark died in the Flood. Their quick burial turned many of them into fossils.

CONQUERED to Extinction

After the Flood, dinosaurs had trouble living in the new world. Climate change and hunting by humans decreased their numbers until they eventually disappeared.

CAPTURED in Fables

Humans recorded encounters with reptile beasts called dragons. But these dragons look and sound a lot like dinosaurs.

COLLECTED from Flood Fossils

Because of fossil discoveries, we're learning more about dinosaurs all the time. Soft tissues inside dinosaur bones support the Bible's claim that dinosaurs and humans walked the earth at the very same time only thousands of years ago.

Dinos and the Gospel

Dinosaurs give us a glimpse of God's incredible creation power. But their fossils also remind us of the sickness, disease, death, and judgment that entered the world through Adam's sin. And these sad things continue to this very day. Can you think of someone you know who is sick, or hurt, or lonely? Many people in this world are separated from God by the sin in their hearts. Will it always be this way?

"For God so loved the world that He gave His only begotten Son, that whoever believes in Him should not perish but have everlasting life." (John 3:16)

Thankfully, the answer is no! God has a special plan to fix all that has gone wrong because of sin. Since the punishment for sin is death, God sent His Son, Jesus, to take that punishment for us. That's why Jesus died such a terrible death on the cross!

But He didn't stay dead. God brought Him back to life! And at the right time, He'll fix all that is broken in the world. If you put your trust in Jesus, someday you will live in His new world, a world even better than the one He first created with people and dinosaurs. You can live forever with the One who made you! Isn't that amazing news?

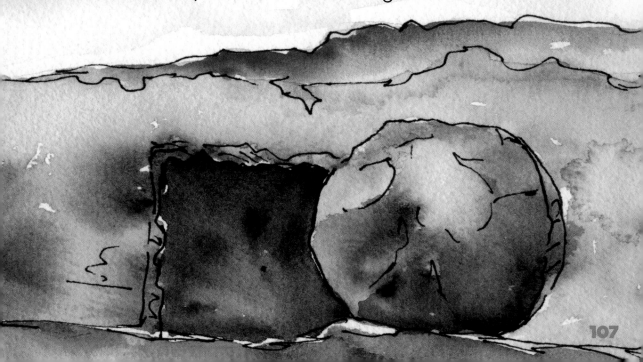

Dino Resources to Help You Dig Deeper

For more detailed answers to your dinosaur and creation questions, visit ICR.org. Search for these articles and other news describing the latest scientific research. Dino books and DVDs are offered in our online store (ICR.org/store).

Articles

"Were Dinosaurs on Noah's Ark?" Brian Thomas, M.S.

"How Could All the Animals Get On Board Noah's Ark?" John D. Morris, Ph.D.

"*T. Rex* Toddler Answers Noah's Ark Questions," Brian Thomas, M.S.

"Settling the Dinosaur Weight Debate," Tim Clarey, Ph.D., and Jeffrey P. Tomkins, Ph.D.

"What's It Like to Dig for Dinosaur Bones?" Brian Thomas, M.S.

"Did Some Dinosaurs Really Have Feathers?" Frank Sherwin, M.A., and Brian Thomas, M.S.

"Scientist Stumped by Actual Dinosaur Skin," Brian Thomas, M.S.

"Mummified Dinosaur Skin Looks Young," Brian Thomas, M.S.

"New Fossil Dubbed 'Platypus Dinosaur,'" Brian Thomas, M.S.

"Did Humans Cause Dinosaur Extinctions?"
Brian Thomas, M.S.

"What Would Need to Change for a Dinosaur to Evolve into a Bird?" John D. Morris, Ph.D.

"Dinosaur Soft Tissues: They're Real!" Brian Thomas, M.S.

"Did Dinosaurs Survive the Flood?" John D. Morris, Ph.D.

Books

Guide to Dinosaurs

Dinosaurs and the Bible

Guide to Creation Basics

Dinosaurs: Marvels of God's Design

DVDs

Uncovering the Truth about Dinosaurs

Dinosaurs on Display: A Fossil Walk with the Beasts of the Earth

Discovering Dinosaurs: Five Details from Fossils and History

Unlocking the Mysteries of Genesis, Episode 7

Glossary

Ark The floating box (boat) God told Noah to build so he, his family, and air-breathing, land-living animals could survive the Flood.

Behemoth A huge creature God talks about in the book of Job. It fits the description of a Long-Neck Dino.

Bony plates Flat pieces of bone that extend from the body of a dinosaur. They're often found with fossils of Plated Lizards like *Stegosaurus*.

Carnivore A meat-eating animal.

Circular reasoning Using the very thing you're trying to prove as evidence of its truth.

Coelacanth A large, deep-ocean fish. Evolution scientists said it went extinct before its descendants supposedly evolved into humans, but it was discovered alive in 1938.

Collagen A protein that gives strength and flexibility to body tissues. Found in some dinosaur fossils and other fossils.

Creation scientist A scientist who believes in biblical creation; a scientist who believes Genesis is history.

Crest A ridge along the top of a bone. Crests in dinosaurs like *Parasaurolophus* were hollow and possibly used to make sounds.

Cretaceous A system of sedimentary rock layers that contain specific grains, muds, and fossil types like *T. rex*. These are the upper-level dinosaur Flood rocks.

Dragon Dinosaur-like creature depicted in ancient art and described by famous people in history.

Elastin A highly elastic protein that allows many tissues in the body to keep their shape after stretching or contracting. Found in some dinosaur fossils.

Evolution The theory that every creature formed from one original creature through small changes over millions of years.

Extinct When a plant or animal has no living members.

Fall An event described in Genesis in which Adam and Eve sinned in the Garden of Eden and God cursed the world with death.

Flood An event described in the Bible in which God covered the entire Earth with water as punishment for evil.

Fossil The remains of a creature that has been preserved in rock. When many fossils are found buried together, it's called a fossil graveyard.

Frill Extra skin jutting out from the head or spine. It's found mostly in reptiles and was often supported by bone in ceratopsian dinosaurs.

Gastroliths Small stones swallowed by a bird, reptile, or fish to help grind food for digestion.

Gospel The good news that Jesus died to pay for our sins and rose from the grave to defeat death. If we trust Him, we can know God and live forever with Him.

Habitat The place an animal usually lives.

Ice Age A period after the Flood when some of Earth's water froze into broad sheets of ice on many land surfaces. The ice lasted for hundreds of years.

Jurassic A system of sedimentary rock layers found beneath Cretaceous system rocks in places where both systems occur. It contains certain rock types and fossils such as *Diplodocus*. These are the mid-level dinosaur Flood rocks.

Land bridges Strips of land that connected continents and allowed animals and people to migrate around the world during the Ice Age.

Living fossil A plant or animal that is rediscovered after it was thought to be extinct and known only from its fossils.

Marginocephalia A group of plant-eating dinosaurs with a frill at the back of their skulls. Includes dinos like *Triceratops* and *Pachycephalosaurus*.

Marine reptiles Reptiles that lived in the ocean. Some examples are mosasaurs, ichthyosaurs, and plesiosaurs.

Ornithopoda A group of plant-eating dinosaurs with beaks and no body armor. Includes dinos like *Iguanodon* and *Brachylophosaurus*.

Osteoderms Plates of bone embedded in reptile skin to form extra-tough scales. They're found in Armor Dinos, as well as some marine reptiles, alligators, and frogs.

Predator A hunting animal that feeds on other animals.

Prey An animal that is hunted and killed for food.

Radiocarbon A rare type of carbon atom that releases particles and radiation until it stabilizes into a nitrogen atom. Used to estimate ages of recently deposited carbon-containing objects like wood, coal, or bone.

Reptile A cold-blooded vertebrate animal that has dry, scaly skin without fur or feathers and lays eggs on land. Some examples include dinosaurs, snakes, lizards, crocodiles, turtles, and tortoises.

Sauropodomorpha A group of extremely large plant-eating dinosaurs with long necks, long tails, and small heads. Includes dinos like *Diplodocus* and *Brachiosaurus*.

Scales Thickened folds of reptile skin that often have small disks of hard protein or bone inside.

Sin Disobeying God.

Soft tissue Animal body parts—made by cells or made of cells—that flex when they're bent. Examples include skin, blood vessels, and tendons. Rare fossils contain partly decayed soft tissues.

Species A group of similar plants or animals that can interbreed.

Tasmanian devil A small, ferocious, meat-eating marsupial with mostly black fur and a long tail. It lives only in Tasmania.

Theropoda A group of two-leg, sharp-tooth dinosaurs with three-toed feet. Includes dinos like *T. rex* and *Velociraptor*.

Thyreophora A group of armored or plated plant-eating dinosaurs. Includes dinos like *Stegosaurus* and *Ankylosaurus*.

Vegetarian A plant-eating animal or human.

Index

S

Sauropelta, 94

Sauropodomorpha, 13, 70, 73, 75, 77, 79

scale(s), 39, 52, 98

Sharp-Tooth Dino(s), 13, 56, 60-61, 84

skin, 38-39, 50, 52, 94, 98

skull(s), 24, 49, 60, 72, 81-82, 88, 98

soft tissue(s), 38, 50, 105

spike(s), spiky; 66, 88, 90, 92, 94, 100

spine, 24, 68-69, 102

Spinosaurus, 20, 68

Stegosaurus, 58, 66, 91-92

stomach, 26, 72, 102

swamp(s), 22, 33

T

tail(s), 12, 26, 57, 66, 70, 72, 74, 76, 81, 86, 90, 92, 94

Team Veggie, 20, 72, 74, 76, 78, 82, 84, 86, 88, 92, 94, 98, 100, 102

Theropoda, 13, 60, 63, 65, 67, 69

theropods, 50

Thyreophora, 13, 90, 93, 95

tooth, teeth; 14-15, 20, 24, 40, 62, 64, 66, 72, 82, 84, 88, 92, 94, 96-98, 101-102

tracks, 39

Triceratops, 49, 80, 82, 84

Tyrannosaurus rex, T. rex; 20, 24, 38, 57, 60, 62, 82, 90

V

vegetarian(s), 20, 31

Velociraptor, 60, 64, 84

vertebrae, 66, 72

Contributors

 **Susan Windsor** is the graphic designer and illustrator for the Institute for Creation Research. Her background as a watercolor artist came in handy to develop this book. Her favorite dinosaur is the *Stegosaurus*.

 **Christy Hardy** is a writer and editor for ICR. As a kid scientist, she used to dig for dino bones with a spoon in her neighbor's backyard. Her favorite dinosaur is the *Spinosaurus*.

 **Truett Billups** is a writer and editor for ICR. His favorite candy is Mamba, and his favorite dinosaur is the *Torosaurus*.

Michael Stamp is a writer and editor for ICR. He also writes Christian novels. His favorite dinosaur is the *Triceratops*.

Brian Thomas is a science researcher and writer for ICR. He is an expert in biotechnology and dino soft tissues. None of his five teenagers show the same interest in dinosaurs as he does...yet. His favorite dinosaur is the one he's currently studying.

Jayme Durant is the Director of Communications and Executive Editor for ICR. As the mom of four kids, she's stepped on her share of toy dinos on the living room floor. Her favorite dinosaur today is the *Brachiosaurus*.

Thank You

A special thank you to Dr. Tim Clarey for his careful review of this book. His expertise in dinosaurs and geology proved invaluable as we sought to accurately represent ICR's commitment to solid science and biblical creation.

We'd also like to thank ICR's CEO Dr. Henry M. Morris III for his support throughout the development of this project, his biblical expertise, and his thorough review of this book.

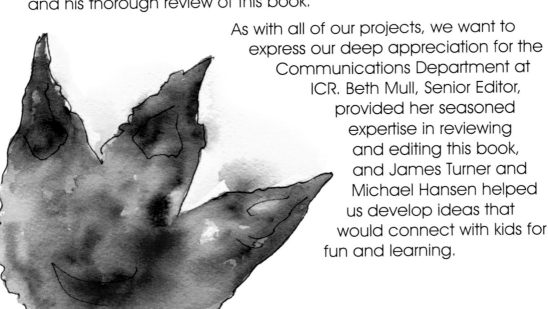

As with all of our projects, we want to express our deep appreciation for the Communications Department at ICR. Beth Mull, Senior Editor, provided her seasoned expertise in reviewing and editing this book, and James Turner and Michael Hansen helped us develop ideas that would connect with kids for fun and learning.

About ICR

At the Institute for Creation Research, we want you to know God's Word can be trusted with everything it speaks about—from how and why we were made, to how the universe was formed, to how we can know God and receive all He has planned for us.

To build your faith, our scientists have spent decades researching how science supports what the Bible says. Our experts earned degrees in many different fields, including genetics, biotechnology, astronomy, astrophysics, physics, nuclear physics, zoology, geology, medicine, public health, theology, and engineering.

In addition to our books, we publish a monthly *Acts & Facts* magazine, a quarterly *Days of Praise* devotional, and loads of scientific articles online. We also produce DVD series on science and the Bible, and our scientists travel across the country to speak at events and share their findings. For more information on our ministry, please visit our website, ICR.org.

Other Dino Resources

GUIDE TO
DINOSAURS
ICR
INSTITUTE FOR CREATION RESEARCH

DINOSAURS
AND THE
BIBLE

BRIAN THOMAS

THE SCIENCE OF THE
BIBLICAL ACCOUNT

DR. TIM CLAREY

DINOSAURS
...ELS OF GOD'S DESIGN

UNCOVERING THE TRUTH ABOUT DINOSAURS

UNCOVERING
THE TRUTH
ABOUT DINOSAURS

EXPLORE THE MO...
MYSTERIO...

ICR
INSTITUTE FOR CREATION RESEARCH
TRUTH ON TOUR

DINOSAURS ON DISPLAY
A FOSSIL WALK WITH THE
BEASTS OF THE EARTH

ICR
INSTITUTE FOR CREATION RESEARCH
TRUTH ON TOUR

DISCOVERING DINOSAURS
FIVE DETAILS FROM
FOSSILS AND HISTORY

Brian Thomas

1
2
DINOSAURS AND DRAGONS
UNCOVERING
THE TRUTH
ABOUT DINOSAURS
3
DINOSAURS AND...
4
THE HARD TRUTH
UNCOVERING
THE TRUTH
ABOUT DINOSAURS

Digging Into
Dinosaurs

Episode

ICR.org/store

Family Resources from ICR

- 12-episode DVD series
- Family-friendly, multi-age level
- Includes a 112-page viewer guide
- Addresses the most popular creation topics

ICR.org/store

Family Resources from ICR

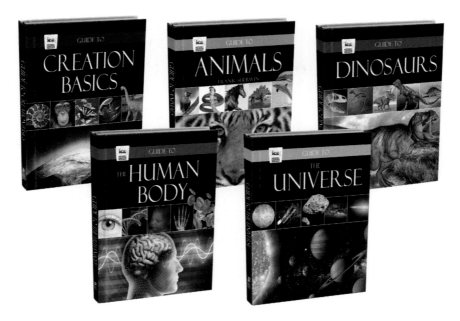

- Family-friendly, multi-age-level book series
- Packed with fun illustrations
- Hardbound, full color
- Trusted biblical creation message

ICR.org/store